Dear Me
The Art of Loving Yourself

Personal Growth / Self-Help

YENIFFER R. GONZÁLEZ MOLERO

This book is an English translated copy of the original book *"Querida yo el arte de amarte"*.

Contact : libroelartedeamarte@gmail.com
Instagram : @yeniffergonzalezz
www.yeniffergonzalezz.com

ISBN: 979-8-9889953-2-6

To my partner, my family, my friends, and all those who made my life a space of learning.

Thank you, Carlos, for supporting me in my projects. You helped me get out of my comfort zone; you motivated me to look for those things that make my heart glimmer. Thank you for your daily love and understanding, for your tender kisses and thank you for working on you offering me the best version of you, for listening to me, for your care, for spoiling me and for accompanying me on this road we call life.

I love you, piojito.

INDEX

DEAR ME

From: Me
To: Me

*T*he past: a story that has passed. Don't look at it with pain or regret, rather, look at it as a steppingstone, as stories that made you learn, moments that taught you to step out of your comfort zone. Many times, you felt overwhelmed with the desire to give it all up but look at you here today, writing what could be your first book, a book that not only talks about your personal and professional growth but one that is directed to all those people who, like you, someday need to see the light, a book that has the purpose of improving the lives of those who need love. This new stage of your life makes you feel proud and embrace that little girl who once daydreamed of helping others.

Dear me, if this were my last day of life, I would have to tell you that I am so proud of you. I love you more than anything in this world. There are so many stories, I could write dozens of books. This book is not about my stories, but about how I overcame all those moments that made me feel defeated, that filled me with darkness, that extinguished my smile and my desire to live.

Who knew that you could endure pain and see life in the brightest of colors.

To you, dear reader, I would like to say: if you are going through difficult times, riddled with darkness, after practicing the techniques I share in this book, you will be able to see life differently – trust me!

We live in a society in which bad news are part of our daily routine. Consumed by social networks, but without socializing with reality, we hide behind a screen and appear, many times, to have a life that we don't really have. Although I don't see it so dark, I guess many of us, use this medium as a form of distraction and want to share the beautiful things that happen to us. And sure, that's fine. However, we spend many hours glued to the screens, which affects us personally, professionally, and especially psychologically. Because we often start to compare ourselves with everybody else and question our own life; that's when the world falls apart.

Dedicating time to working on yourself, building your best version, and healing your wounds is and will be the best and most beautiful journey you will ever take in your life. Self-knowledge won't be an easy task, but I assure you it will be worth it.

“ The worst loneliness is not feeling comfortable with yourself.

MARK TWAIN

1

MY CHILDHOOD AND TEENAGE YEARS

Abuse, harassment, bullying and trauma

D ear reader, I'd like share a little of my story with you. It is extremely difficult for me to talk about my life and expose myself to the world in this way. Although I accept my past, because I value its teachings, it still is something hard for me to talk about. Talking about my past makes me feel vulnerable, however, I feel that only by knowing my story you will truly understand why I wrote this book.

My name is Yeniffer Rossana González Molero. I was born in Maracaibo, in the state of Zulia in Venezuela and I am currently thirty years old. I consider myself a lover of knowledge. I am also an HSP (a highly sensitive person), which makes me have excellent qualities, but, as with everything in life, it has its cons – being highly sensitive can affect me emotionally more than it does others.

I was raised in a very large family with divorced parents, I have one older brother and six half-siblings, and I would say that I was mainly raised by my great-grandmother and my maternal grandmother, as well as my aunts, who were an essential part of my growing up. Even though my parents rebuilt their lives with new partners and had new children, I always saw them as one extended family, I grew up loving them all the same. I had an old-fashioned upbringing, filled with values and principles such as respect for elders. Since I was a child, I was ambitious, I was always eager to learn new things and dreamed of helping humanity. In some way, I felt that helping others was my life purpose. I guess I learned that from my maternal grandmother; seeing her empathy and love for others, always helping her mother, siblings, and all those who needed her. I always witnessed the unconditional love that she indirectly planted in me.

I still have some funny memories from when I was in kindergarten, when I must have been between three and five years old. I loved to use play dough to make long nails and I used to put aluminum cans (as high heels) on my shoes, until one day, while I was walking and showing my play dough nails to my classmates, I tripped and fell. Because I hit my head, I got a huge bump, and that was the last time I ever used aluminum cans as heels (ha, ha, ha).

BULLYING AND TRAUMA

Not all my memories are as funny as that last one, though, my life wasn't always that sweet. I'll share a little more about that. As I grew up, I asked myself a lot of questions: why did my parents separate? Why couldn't I have a united and happy family? Why did my grandmothers end up raising me? Why did my mother work tirelessly, without spending ever time with us? Why didn't my father help my mother? Why did she leave me to my own devices, in the hands of my great-grandmother, after my mother rebuilt her life? And why was it that I was left to my great-grandmother? These were a lot of questions for a child, and to make the story a little more dramatic, my brother and I often suffered physical abuse from my great-grandmother. When I was a child, I felt a lot of resentment for the way we were being raised, but now, as an adult and from the standpoint of forgiveness, I can understand that my great-grandmother only replicated what she had been taught and had experienced herself in her life.

When we were less than ten years old, my brother and I were on the verge of running away from home. We often questioned our lives and even fantasized about committing suicide. We didn't want to be abused anymore. Although the abuse I received can't compare to the abuse my brother received, I remember that she would beat him with anything she could get her hands on, whether it was sticks, ropes, hoses, belts, etc. We suffered grave consequences if we didn't listen to my great-grandmother, who threatened to hit us harder if we told my parents about it. But who was going to believe us, my brother and I thought, if our parents practically abandoned us?

My father rarely saw us, only on special occasions, such as birthdays or Christmas. On those dates, everything was very nice. My brother and I received the love we lacked during the whole year. He would give us presents, buy us clothes, and take us for a walk. Only then did we remember that we were children. My mother worked a lot and loved on us in her free time. Although she spent very little time with us, she made us feel loved. I guess this was normal, being a single mother of two children.

We were growing up with our grandmothers, while my mother was with her husband and new children, and my father with his wife and his new family. When my brother became a little rebellious, my mother decided it would be best to send him to live with my father for a while, not knowing the hell my brother would go through. He continued to be mistreated, but this time by my father, who affected his self-esteem with words such as: "You're good for nothing", "You can't do anything right", "Grow up, you're useless", among many others. The after-effects of this psychological abuse affect him to this day, and he continues to work on them. Obviously, that was not the best way to raise my brother, but who am I to judge my father when he didn't have his father's support growing up either?

I, on the other hand, moved back to my mother's house to finish my last years of school. In my first year of high school, I went back to live with my grandmother. After that, I lived with my father for a year while I was in my second year of high school (it was the first and last time I lived with my father). And finally (from third to fifth year of high school), I went back to live at my grandmother's house. Practically, every year I lived in a different place.

Days turned into years, and my great-grandmother had already aged, she was lying in bed unable to move, with Alzheimer's and plagued with other physical illnesses. It was then that I learned to forgive from the heart, without her ever asking for it. I began to feel compassion for a person who had been cruel to me. Regardless of all the harm she had done to us, I cared for her, showered her, prayed for her, slept next to her, and fed her until the day she died. This experience taught me that we judge our caregivers by the way they raise us, I never did and never will agree with teaching by mistreatment, but I understood that many of my family members were raised that way and as a consequence, followed the same pattern.

Others, on the other hand, decided to change and end the violence. In the end, we were the generation that stopped that kind of abuse. Today, we are more conscious of how we teach and address others with respect.

❝❝I am more than my scars.

ANDREW DAVIDSON

My brother and I were bullied a lot growing up: he was bullied because he had strabismus and needed glasses, and I was bullied because I was the tallest and thinnest of my classmates. We were teased so much that I couldn't take it anymore. I remember one day when I was in my classroom and the teacher had gone out for a moment, the children started to make fun of me, yelling: "Broomstick, giraffe, *Mariapalito*, Betty Spaghetty, light post!" All for being very thin and taller than the rest. I remember that I got so angry I suffered a fit of rage and started to lift all the chairs and tables in the classroom with great force. Thankfully, I didn't hurt anyone, but everyone was paralyzed (I still remember their faces), no one expected me to react that way. At that moment, the teacher arrived and when she saw the whole room in disarray, she took me to the principal's office. After calming down, I was able to explain what had happened; the teacher and the principal believed me. How could they not? I used to be a very quiet and studious child, they had never had any complaints about me, so they didn't file a report and they made sure that the other children behaved well.

To clear my mind, when I felt overwhelmed or sad, I had the habit of going up to the roof of my house. There, no one would see me cry, I would also go up there to look at the sky, read, draw, or study. It was my safe place, where I felt at peace. I had a white notebook that my mother had given me on one of my birthdays, she had made it with her own hands... just for me. I used it as a diary (to let off steam), I drew characters to give life to my stories and it helped me feel better. Here, I could finally be myself.

As a result of the bullying, I had very low self-esteem. I remember one night going with my aunt and my cousins to a 15th birthday party. I felt very sad. I didn't like the way I looked and, secretly, I started to cry. My aunt saw me and took me with her to her room in private: "Why are you crying?" she asked. I explained that I didn't feel pretty because of my thinness and height. She lovingly lifted my face, took my hand, and said looking me in the eyes: "Yeni, you are beautiful, you are intelligent, you are good, look at me... I am very short, what you have too much of, maybe I lack, I have to wear very high heels and even then, I don't reach your height. I am so short that I have to use stairs to reach some things on the shelf, and you, you don't have that problem. If I were as tall as you, I assure you that I would love every extra inch. Being taller than the rest doesn't make you ugly, it makes you different — it even gives you abilities that others don't have. Don't ever let anyone make you feel bad for being different, because being different makes you unique". I will never forget those words: that was my first lesson in self-esteem.

" Everyone is strange. We should all celebrate our

individuality and not be ashamed of it.

JOHNNY DEPP

When I was nine years old, I had to move to another city with my mother. At the new school, I already felt better about myself. Nobody made fun of me, I loved studying. At the age of ten, I was already representing the school in sports and art, even won a trophy in ball throwing, and was recognized for my paintings. At the age of eleven, I belonged to the most popular dance group, which made me feel more confident. Here, I made some very good friendships that I still keep today.

ABUSE AND HARASSMENT

But to this day, I am still working on my past wounds. During my life, I went through several instances of sexual abuse and harassment. Some classmates wanted to experiment and did not know the consequences, I didn't even know them myself. One day I was harassed by several of my classmates at school, who forcibly grabbed me so that one of them touched my private parts and kissed me. I tried to defend myself at all costs, managed to get away, and punched one of them in the face right when the bell rang, and luckily, I managed to escape.

As a teenager, I was diagnosed with a spinal problem and was referred to physical therapy. I went to see several doctors. My grandmother went to the appointments with me, and stayed in the waiting room while I went in for my therapies. My therapist was very nice. Until one day, while I was in his office, he asked me to take off my clothes and lie down on the table for a massage. I felt uncomfortable and told him that I didn't need to undress, since the massage would be on my back, and that I could pull up my shirt as I had done on every other occasion – that should have been enough. He took me by the arms and cornered me against the wall, trying to kiss me. I begged him to let go. He kept telling me to calm down and told me nothing that I didn't want would happen. I replied that if he didn't let go, I was going to scream as loud as I could, until someone heard me. At that point he let me go, I grabbed my things and walked out of the room.

Years later, as an adult, I started working. A friend of mine had gotten me a position as an administrative assistant in a technology company. The first few days, the owner, my boss, was very friendly to me. Every day, he would wait for me in the office, and show me my daily tasks. It was a training class. Every time he would come up to me while I was working on the computer, he would whisper in my ear how pretty I looked. Since I needed the work and didn't want to make my friend look bad, I kept going even though I was distraught. At that time, I did not know the laws and there was not enough information regarding workplace harassment. I vividly remember the last day. As usual, my boss was waiting for me in the office, he no longer whispered only how pretty I looked, but added: "Yeni, I like you very much and I would like to see you outside of work". I still remember how my fast my heart was beating and how nervous he made me feel, my palms were sweating. I told him I would think about it and give him an answer the next day. He agreed.

That was the last day I worked for him. I never went back there again.

Can you imagine what it's like to be doing your job and have your boss come up to you and whisper in your ear how much he likes you? I'm telling you; it was disgusting.

In those years of my life, I became very fearful, I could not trust men. I was afraid of having to expose myself to them. I felt that I attracted a lot of attention, so I started to dress in baggy clothes and to have a masculine personality, I felt that this was the only way I could protect myself. I lived in constant fear, every day I would go out in the street hoping that nothing bad would happen to me.

I have never told anyone about these experiences, much less my family. I was so afraid they wouldn't believe me. I guess I thought that if I told anyone, things would get worse. And I experienced many more of those harassments in my life. Now, as an adult I realize that the words my great-grandmother used to say, "No one will believe you, if you say something about it, it will get worse". They marked me so strongly and got into my head so much that I truly believed them. I regret not having said anything at the time– perhaps other girls would have benefitted from my story and had not been lucky enough to escape like I had done so many times.

I can't turn back time, and if I could, maybe I would make the same mistakes again, because experiences are what make you grow and learn. Unfortunately, I was naïve; an insecure and easily manipulated child. Now that I have lived and that I can raise my voice about these topics, I am writing this book that I would have loved to read when I was a teenager. I wish I had had the tools available today, access to information and more general acceptance of psychological therapies.

It was hard growing up and hearing comments from other people without knowing all that I have gone through to get to where I am.

"Everything comes easy to you because you are pretty, surely you don't have to work hard to get things done. You are always positive, surely you have a perfect life. Yeniffer doesn't complain about anything because she is always doing well". I hope this book will make you realize that a smiling face doesn't necessarily mean a perfect life.

> " Dear past me, forgive me, for all the times I told you that you could do it on your own, when you actually needed help.

YENIFFER GONZALEZ

My five years of high school were the best years of my Teenage Years. I focused on getting very good grades and also represented the school in sports and art. I belonged to the discipline club (we kept order among the students), and the environmental care group. Everyone knew and respected me, it was beautiful. I made very good friendships that I still have kept to this day. I won awards in poetry and for the best academic average.

When I graduated from high school, I received a scholarship from the state to study business administration and I was granted the AMA project (Admission by Academic Merit) to enter the University of Zulia State, LUZ, one of the best universities in the country, where I began to study

Geodesic Engineering. Two years later, the country started having serious problems. There were strikes against the government, the atmosphere was tense and dangerous, and since the university was very far from my home, I decided to change careers and take the state scholarship to study business administration at the UNIR Institute, a technological university that was closer to where I lived. Months later, I started working and as a consequence, I missed classes at the university, so they took away my scholarship, but that didn't stop me. With what I earned at my job I could pay for college. I rearranged my schedule with *Farmatodo Sur*, the company I worked for; the managers were very fond of me, and with their help, I was able to return to my studies, but, this time, I only went to college on Fridays and Saturdays all day. This stage of my life was exhausting. I had no time for anything but work and study. I remember that I slept very little, ate very poorly, and did not socialize with anyone, but in the end, I made it, I finished my degree and graduated as a Higher University Technician in Administration, in 2016.

I just turned thirty. As I write this book it's July 2023. I look back and I can see how amazing my life has been over the past few years, but if I stop to think, I can also see a lot of pain. There are very sad parts of my life that I will not publish here. I want to clarify that, while I was growing up, I read a lot of self-help books and as an adult, I attended psychological therapies. I was given answers to all those questions that disturbed me since I was a child.

"It's okay to feel bad and sad if you're going through a hard

time. Validate your emotions
and give yourself the love you
didn't receive then.

YENIFFER GONZALEZ

I share my story, not to make you feel sorry for me, but to make you look at yourself in a mirror and know that after any storm, the sun always shines, sometimes even behind a beautiful rainbow. I learned that not all men are evil, that the experiences I had to live could have happened to anyone, and that I could not be afraid to live, because this life is worth living.

I once heard a speech that I liked very much, from a woman talking about the male gender. It went something like: *"A man does not rape, a rapist rapes"*, *"A man does not kill, a murderer kills"*, *"A man does not abuse, an abuser abuses"*, *"A man does not humiliate, a coward humiliates"*, *"Violence has no gender"*, *"Men are not bad because they are men"*, *"Violence cannot be generalized or pigeonholed as if all evil and abuse were of the male gender"*. This made a lot of sense to me, because I am also the daughter of a man, I have brothers, uncles, cousins, and a grandfather.

I'll tell you a little ahead of time; today, my siblings are grown up, some of them have children and live in other countries. My parents are single again, each living their own lives. I talk to my grandmother, my father, and my mother on WhatsApp every day, as they are the ones who keep me updated about my family. They have all grew and evolved dramatically. My relationship with my family became a core of love and respect, my mom is my best friend today, my relationship with my dad improved and my grandma is still the apple of my eyes. Currently, it's been over six years without seeing my family, I have been living from one country to another, moving around the world, like many other immigrants, my dreams packed in my suitcase. Between tears I can tell you, that I do not lose faith, I know that soon I will be embracing my family again.

2

BEAUTY PAGEANTS AND PROFESSIONAL MODELING

The stories no one shares

INSTITUTIONAL TITLE

Here begins another stage of my life. It is a long story, so I will summarize it as best as I can. When I was in college (UNIR), I had a lot of influence from my professor Sobeida Gonzalez, who taught me the subject of legislation. She and my classmates wanted me to participate in a beauty pageant that would be held at the university; in Venezuela, beauty contests are a proud event, so they managed to convince me.

While I was participating, there was a lot of drama, I had no time for anything. While I worked and studied, I was also attending the contest rehearsals. It was crazy. Each girl represented a career, although I was studying administration, I had to represent the psychopedagogy career, because the contest they were already advanced when I entered, and the administration career was represented by Andrea, whom I later became friends with. I remember that there was a lot of internal controversy in the contest, it was whispered that the jury had a favorite; a girl singer who was known for having participated in a famous program in the country. It was rumored that since the judges were her friends, she would have an advantage. The rest of the girls and I disagreed, as we felt it was unfair for the judges to know the contestant, we demanded that the judges be changed and threatened to leave if they didn't. The event coordinator agreed and changed the jury. On the day of the show, the contestants arrived at the place, our makeup artists and stylists put our makeup, we got dressed and it began. We did our presentations, dances, and we modeled the gala dress – I never imagined that I would be the winner of the Miss Elegance sash! Andrea and I were the finalists. Holding hands tightly, we waited for the jury's final result. It was a big surprise for me to hear my name when they called out the winner of the contest, because even though I felt I had good qualities to win, I was competing with beautiful and well-prepared women, and I had no prior experience in beauty pageants. However, I was crowned, and I became *CHICA UNIR* 2014. The participants were happy and congratulated me. I remember taking off my crown and with the microphone in hand, I dedicated the triumph to them, I told them that the crown was for all of them and that we had all won. In addition to the title, I won a beautiful memory of that experience and few new friends. I never thought that would be the beginning of my career as a beauty queen.

After winning that institutional contest, I started attending a small agency for models called *Ariel Producciones*, where I received a lot of support from the coordinators, Israel, Patricia, Joselin, Ranssel and my colleagues.

" Celebrate your own victories, because no one else really understands what it took you to achieve them.

ANONYMOUS

REGIONAL TITLE

The following year, I participated in another pageant. This time, it was a state one, thanks to the influence of my aunt Emmy, who believed in me and supported me every step of the way. Out of hundreds of girls from Zulia and Falcon State, I was selected along with thirty-eight girls as the official candidate for Miss Nor Occidental 2015.

After months of preparation, the day of the contest arrived; it was a day I will never forget. Although now I remember it with grace because I understood that life had a lesson prepared for me, which at that moment I did not expect.

I was at my father's house. I got up very early to go to the designer to pick up my gala dress, as I had my last fitting for the final night. My father's car had broken down, so he told me to go and grab a cab. As I did, I noticed that there was no one on the streets, except for a couple of motorized. My intuition told me that something was happening, but, as I had no choice, I kept walking. When I arrived at the corner, I was greeted by the motorized, pointing a gun at me, ordering me to give up my phone. I nervously told them that I did not have one. I took it out and gave it to them, but first I asked them to give me back the storage chip, I told them that I needed it – how awful, what was I thinking – they did not pay attention to me, instead, they pointed the gun at me again and simply left. I froze for a minute and then went back to my father's house. When I arrived with tears in my eyes, my father opened the door; he imagined what had happened, so he put on his shoes and went to find a cab with me. I took the cab hoping to get to my designer's house, but I never made it, because the address was saved in my cell phone, and I didn't remember it. I gave up and prayed to the universe that my designer would show up at the place of the show.

I arrived at the Lía Bermúdez Art Center in Maracaibo, where the contest was to be held. My dear Isidro Linares started to do my makeup. After spending the day in between makeup, rehearsals, interviews, etc., my designer, Jonathan Navil, arrived. He told me that he had been trying to contact me all day, and I told him what happened with my cell phone. We went to the bathroom to try on my dress. Fortunately, the dress fit me perfectly. It was beautiful, just as I had dreamed it would be. He told me that he would no longer dress another of the candidates for whom he had also made a dress, because that morning he had chosen another designer, so I still had both dresses at my disposal. Both were beautiful, mine was red with a sexy leg opening, and the other dress was turquoise, covering me down to my feet. I loved my dress and had even bought some red velvet heels to match it.

The event started, we did our opening show, then our presentation. We modeled in swimsuit, and when it was our turn to do the modeled in gala dress, I realized that my red velvet heels were not where I had left them. They had been hidden or stolen; I didn't understand why someone would want to do something like that to me. I was always a very good companion with all the girls. Since I had no more time to "worry" and it was my turn to go out, I had to "get busy" and keep wearing the only heels I had and that I had already worn during the whole show, they were not pretty and did not match my red dress, so my designer and I, decided to go for the turquoise dress, since it covered my shoes.

Too many bad things had happened to me during the day. I was not going to let myself be defeated, so I went out with my face high and the confidence of a winner.

Can you guess what happened?

I was awarded the Chica Garbo sash and crowned Miss Nor Occidental 2015!

Along with six other girls, I was one of the winners to participate in the Miss Venezuela selection, representing the State of Zulia and Falcon. I couldn't believe it – I had made it!

Today, I still wonder who stole my red heels (ha, ha, ha).

NATIONAL TITLE

Winning Miss Nor Occidental 2015 gave me the key to preparing myself and participating in the Miss Venezuela pageant selection. I moved to the capital, Caracas, where my paternal family lived: my grandfather, my aunts, and Jacqueline, my grandfather's wife. They supported me, opened their home, and cared for me. I have so much to thank them for!

That same year, I had to undergo breast implant surgery and a rhynoplasty. It was a difficult decision. I didn't want to do it, but according to my "representative" I needed to have those surgeries, to have a chance to be selected in Miss Venezuela. I also enrolled in the academy "Universidad de la Belleza Gisselle's", to learn oratory and catwalk. I started going to the gym and they put me on a special diet. Those were months of hard preparation.

When the day came to select the candidates for Miss Venezuela 2015, the event was broadcast live and nationally on the Venevisión channel. I was very nervous, surrounded by hundreds of beautiful girls sitting in a giant room waiting to be on the screen. After a while it was my turn, we were six girls representing the states of Zulia and Falcon. We did a presentation dance and waited for the decision of the president of the contest, that time Osmel Sousa. At the end of our presentation there was a few minutes of silence, after which, I heard him say: "The winner and only representative of the State of Zulia, will be Miss... Yeniffer Gonzalez".

I swear I froze; my brain went blank. Trembling, I walked over to the presenter, Leonardo Villalobos, who asked me how I felt about being selected. I couldn't speak, I don't even remember what I said. I never imagined that out of six selected girls from the State contest, plus hundreds of girls coming from different parts of the country, I would be the one who would become one of the 25 candidates for the Miss Venezuela 2015 title. Days after being selected, in another television event, I was awarded the Miss Zulia sash, one more dream come true. I think I dreamed more of wearing the sash of my state on my chest, than winning Miss Venezuela. And for those who don't know, representing the state of Zulia is the greatest pride for any Zulian, because we are very regionalist people. Now that I am writing it, I still can't believe it. It was an incredible experience. I learned a lot and grew professionally. Months of preparation, experiences across the globe. I remember rehearsing the dance and the Miss Venezuela song – an anthem for the whole country on the final night of the contest– when they asked us to listen to the lyrics because they had modified them a little. I sat on the floor while I listened and, with tears in my eyes, I could just believe that I was living my dream of participating in Miss Venezuela. Ever since I was a little girl, I had watched that pageant every year, it was something magical where beautiful women wearing amazing swimsuits and gala dresses participate. Can you imagine? At that moment, I was one of them, I was sitting in one of the rehearsal studios of the most famous program in the whole country. I couldn't believe what I was experiencing and how far I had come. It was amazing.

However, not everything is rosy in these events. I also went through one of the most dramatic experiences of my life. All the candidates are beautiful and intelligent, with great potential to win, really any of them could become the winner, but, as always, there is favoritism, many injustices and also the influence of many powerful people. Many things are rumored, claiming that who knows bribed the jury for a certain girl to win.

While I was there, it was said that some girls were leveraged from some sponsors, that every position within the pageant for the final night was already bought, etc. I was devastated, very upset and disappointed. It bothered me to know that winning was not up to me. I have several personal anecdotes: I received proposals from influential men, who wanted to sleep with me, and said they were willing to pay for my final position. I don't know if they would have really been able to bribe someone from the contest. Anyway, I refused. One of the sponsors wrote me on Instagram claiming he could make me win, but I ignored him and deleted the message. Once while at the gym, the fitness trainer, who I'll call Ronald, called me into his office to assess my weight and measurements – as I assumed at the time, he did with all the girls – and said, "you would have operated on your bigger breasts to look sexier, I could help you a lot to succeed outside this contest." I couldn't believe I was hearing those words from his mouth. I refused and we argued as a result. Ronald started making up rumors about me, bullying me saying I was fat, that I kept eating chocolate. Imagine how that made me feel, after being bullied at school for being thin. Turned out, now I was too fat. I felt very uncomfortable going to that gym and having to see Ronald every day, so I asked Osmel (president of the contest) to let me change the gym. He asked me why, but I did not tell him the truth, because days before I had spoken to another person who told me not to comment on what happened. According to them, Ronald was very influential in the contest and would not let me win. I believed him and lied to the president saying that I had moved to another area, and now the gym was farther away than usual, that I preferred to enroll in the gym at the Lido Hotel, with the trainer Eleazar whom I admired a lot for his work and respect. Osmel was always very respectful with me and accepted my request.

Days later I had an argument with Gisselle (the president of Nor Occidental 2015, and the one in charge of the Miss Venezuela 2015 runway). This affected my situation. According to her, I wasn't following her orders, and I did not deserve the Miss Elegance sash, let alone to win. Did she have the influence to tell me those things? Well, apparently, she did. Her orders were to always dress me, make me up and do my hair the way she wanted me to do it (with bows/buns). I disagreed, because I felt that this was my moment and I had to express my essence. Although many times I followed her requests, a couple of times I refused and wore my hair down, which made us argue. I remember the first "red" gala dress my designer made for me just as I dreamed it; but she changed it, asked him to make me a new dress, because she didn't like the color. When I realized it, there was no turning back. Now, after many years, I think about that moment and I can understand she might have just wanted me to win which is why she was so hard on me so often, but at that moment I felt attacked and manipulated. I was very affected by the comments of the press about my hairstyles: "Zulia always wears her hair up, she should let it down", and that also influenced my feelings.

As a consequence of all the above, I felt that winning was not up to me, so, out of anger and disappointment, I started to eat everything that had been forbidden to me. That was my way of expressing my disagreement. I even gained a few pounds. Even during and after the contest, I began to suffer from body dysmorphia (a *mental disorder characterized by obsessive worry with a perceived defect in physical characteristics*).

On the final night, my gala dress was made by Douglas Tapia, a Zulian designer whom I admired very much. My makeup was done by Andres Eloy and Jose Piña who became my friends and to whom I am very grateful for all the support they gave me.

Before the show started, I felt a helplessness that led me to tears, but I took my strength, put my face up, wiped my tears and got ready to show off that night. I made the decision that no one was going to make me feel bad, I knew I could no longer do anything to win, but I was going to enjoy the final night, because that was the only thing I was going to keep. No one could take away my memories or prevent me from fulfilling that dream I had always had as a child.

The twenty-five candidates did their dances, modeled in swimsuit, and then in the gala dress. Afterwards, we were awarded the special sashes and then the judges chose the finalists. I was chosen among the ten most beautiful women of my country. After the round of questions, the judges chose the winner: the result "ironically" many of us already knew. They crowned "Lara".

Days before, in one of the contests prior to the final night, I had been awarded the Miss Venus Legs sash by national votes. In addition, I gained a lot of personal growth, I was able to assert my decision not to be influenced by others and I defended my state with my values, although that perhaps cost me losing the title of Miss Venezuela. I also kept some good friendships, with whom I shared adventures after the contest.

I want to clarify that I am not sure that the rumors I heard were true. I have no proof that the girls were leveraged by any sponsor, nor that the winners have paid for the crowns. The only thing I am certain of is what I experienced as a participant and that, in the end, every girl was beautiful and intelligent, with or without the help of influential people, really any of us could have won.

And if you were to ask me: "Yeni, if you could go back in time, would you participate again in Miss Venezuela?"

I would say yes, Miss Venezuela is a door to great opportunities.

" I am learning not to feel guilty for setting boundaries, while

being true to what exists within me.

YENIFFER GONZALEZ

INTERNATIONAL PORTFOLIO

I have to admit that competing in Miss Venezuela opened many doors for me. Having represented the State of Zulia, showed my face to the country, as a result, I managed to parade for national and international designers in different runways of Fashion Week worldwide. Many brands and companies wanted to work with me. I also participated in other beauty contests representing Venezuela. I traveled to Ecuador to participate in the CN Models International Search, which was held within the Fashion Week of Ecuador, I modeled for most of the designers and worked hard to make my participation an experience with beautiful memories. I won the award as the best face of the contest, and I was also the winner as the best international model of EFW 2017.

The following year, already living in Miami, Florida, I participated in the Dama Diamante contest, which I also won, becoming Dama Diamante Miami 2018.

Who would have thought that this girl who was bullied so much, would go so far, becoming one of the most beautiful women of her country and representing it worldwide!

> " I feel like I was a caterpillar, that broke its cocoon and became a beautiful butterfly.

YENIFFER GONZALEZ

After all those contests, I continued my career and became a runway model, winning many recognitions that gave me an international portfolio paving my way to get permanent residency in the USA, as an Extraordinary Talent. During my modeling years, I lived in Madrid, Spain, in Miami, Florida and finally in Los Angeles, California.

" Celebrate who you are in your heart of hearts. Love yourself and the world will love you.

AMY LEIGH MERCREE

3

RELATIONSHIPS

Not everything is a fairy tale

This is the part that perhaps many were waiting for. What does Yeniffer tell about her love life? For me, talking about my partners is a very personal subject, because some of them did things that hurt me and others that filled me with happiness. Focusing only on the good would not be telling the whole truth, because regardless of whether I have been happy or not, I learned something from everyone. Some were amazing people and others not so much, but all indirectly pushed me to believe in myself. So, I am going to tell you a little about some of these loves and what I learned from them.

" If you don't see your own value, you will choose people who don't see it either.

MANDY HALE

I will talk about only three people. The first man I want to talk about changed the way I saw my relationships. He lived, slept, and ate with me in mind. At least that's what he made me believe. He indulged me in everything, paid the rent wherever I wanted to live, deposited money monthly in my account, paid all my expenses, took me on trips, treated me like a princess, fulfilled my every wish. We would go on trips on his yacht and even fly in his small plane to other cities to eat and watch the sunset. You may be thinking it was all like a fairy tale. And yes, that's how it made me feel. I thought that lifestyle was only lived in the movies. Everything seemed to be perfect, but of course, everything has its other side: this man was more than twenty years older than me; he had his life figured out, he had previously had a marriage with children, but at that time he was already divorced and wanted to remarry and continue having children. He wanted me to stop working and forget about modeling, to focus only on being his wife. Every day he kept telling me that I didn't need to work because with him, I would have everything. At that time, I did not want to get married, much less have children. The days went by, and we began to argue about those issues on which we did not agree, or rather, we were not going in the same direction. I had already gone through that issue with another ex (which did not end well at all). I could not believe that history was repeating itself, so, without thinking too much about it, I ran away.

You may wonder what I learned from this relationship. I learned that, in the end, it would have been selfish to stay and not fulfill his dream of having a new family, but it would also have been selfish for him to expect me to abandon the profession that I was so passionate about at the time. Love is no fairy tale with a happy ending. Some relationships will only pass through your life to teach you a lesson. This time, I learned that I had to continue building my path.

> " If you are looking for a love that lasts forever, look inside yourself.

ANONYMOUS

Another man I want to share more about was a narcissist I dated. Yes, as you read that right, I fell in love with a narcissist. I didn't know it until the end of the relationship, and you will say: "Yeni, you really have terrible luck". You're right, I thought so too at the time, I laugh about it now. But let me tell you the story:

This man was young, attractive, and intelligent, he could conquer anyone's heart and could convince you of anything he wanted. After a year of long-distance relationship –I lived in Miami, and he lived in Los Angeles – he proposed to me and asked me to move in with him. He convinced me to marry him only under his religion, because according to his beliefs, a man could not live or be with a woman without being married. Unfortunately, I accepted. Spoiler: at the end I found out that, to my luck, that marriage had no legal validity.

That man made my life a living hell when we were already together. He played with my mind, made me think and do things that were not my idea. Immersed in a roller coaster of emotions with extreme ups and downs, he managed to distance myself from my profession, my

31

family, and friends. He forced me to dress as he saw fit, and even to have sex with him, even if I didn't want to, because, according to him, that was the job of a good wife. He kept me like that for three years. It was after much psychological abuse that I realized the damage he was doing to me; he lowered my self-esteem to the floor, making me feel inferior to him and, therefore, making me feel like I needed him. You might ask "Yeni, how did you put up with all those things?" Well... they were not things he did roughly and unconsciously. Narcissists don't feel empathy, so he doesn't suffer regret either. Besides, he was very cunning, and he was getting what he wanted little by little. When we would argue, he would promise me in tears that he would never do it again, he wanted us to fight for our relationship. Although it was hard for me to admit it, I always fell for his manipulation, his fleeting regret convinced me.

He was from a Moroccan and Spanish family that professes Islam (the religion of the Muslims). I learned a lot about this religion and even studied the Koran, its holy book. I liked very much what that religion professes, but I realized that he used it to his convenience, really, he did not follow it, he just hid in it, he tended to use others as a tool for his own purposes.

During our last discussion, we were on vacation in Mallorca, Spain, where his parents lived. He had promised to improve and stop being so possessive and controlling. Everything was going very well, it had been a month without arguments, we were going out with his family and touring the island. One night, returning from the beach, our cell phones were discharged, and I put mine on charge and he asked me for my charger, because it charged faster. I remember telling him to wait for mine to finish charging, but he came every five minutes to see if it was ready and asked me again, and I repeated the same thing. Then, there came a moment when he got so angry that he punched the kitchen door with his fist, causing a hole in it. It was his mother's house, and he didn't care about breaking the door, he didn't even apologize. His mother tried to calm him down, and I was paralyzed, so many thoughts came to me; I wondered if at some point instead of the door it could have been me he punched. That night we slept apart.

The next day, we had plans to go to the beach, with his family, I lied to them telling them that I was feeling sick and preferred to stay home to rest. After convincing them to leave without me, I packed my bags, called my friend Sara who lived nearby and left the house. I remember how my heart was beating so fast, like it would burst out of my chest. Once I was out of the house and feeling safe, I wrote him and his family: "Thank you for the hospitality, but I'm going back to Los Angeles today." I didn't even let them answer, after writing I blocked them and that was the last time, I saw them again.

" You don't have to fall in love with someone to have a spark in your eye, fall in love with you... that spark has real power.

ANONYMOUS

Of course, all that pain could only open my eyes. I know that after hitting rock bottom, the only thing you can do is push yourself with all your strength to get to the surface. When that last relationship ended, my real personal growth began.

> " Loving oneself is the most primal of all survival mechanisms.

KAREN HACKEL

I realized that, during my life, I had been repeating certain patterns with my partners, and I knew that something in me kept doing it. So, I started to study a lot about self-love, I took courses, psychological therapies and, finally, I managed to recover and this time creating my best version, a version that would never go through this kind of pain again. I learned to identify what I really expected from a relationship, what I would never accept again and what I was willing to offer. It took time, but I learned a lot about myself, and I am still learning.

Dear reader, if you have gone through similar experiences, maybe you are afraid to fall in love again. I also reached the point of not believing in love, but have faith, build your best version, work on healing your past wounds, and you will understand that love is the most powerful fuel in the world.

In 2022 I opened the way to the man who owns my heart today. We've been together for a year and a half, we met on a dating *app* called *Bumble*

– I must thank my friend Blanca for that, who was the one who recommended it to me.

Let me tell you a little about this love story. I was on vacation with my cousin Gaby, in Cancun, Mexico, after a week getting to know the Mayan Riviera, it was time to leave. I had to take a flight from Cancun to Mexico City, because my plane was leaving from there to Los Angeles. While waiting for my flight at the airport, I opened a dating app and got a request from a handsome airline pilot. I opened his profile and saw that we shared affinities, so I *matched* him. After talking for a whole day on the app, we realized how much we had in common, exchanged cell phone numbers and social networks, and started dating. But there was a tiny problem: he lived in Cancun, and I lived in Los Angeles, California (a problem that would lead us to a solution).

We started traveling together and getting to know each other better, after a month he proposed me to be his girlfriend in the most romantic way: he took me to see the sunrise flying from a hot air balloon over the pyramids of Teotihuacan, in Mexico, with a giant sign saying: "Do you want to be my girlfriend?" My answer was obvious.

Months passed, we took a trip through Europe for more than forty days, where we got to know each other and complemented each other even more. Although we still lived in different countries, we saw each other every month. I would travel to Mexico to see him, and he would organize trips to see me in different cities. We stayed like this for seven months, until we decided to move in together. I went to his country for a few months. Those were extraordinary months in which we lived many adventures, trips, and experiences. Being a permanent resident of the United States, I couldn't be out of the country for that long, so I had to go back, but he came with me this time. We moved together to San Antonio, Texas, a sweltering city in the summer but with a great history and beautiful places to visit.

We have a very healthy relationship, filled with love and respect. We discuss our concerns and seek ways to understand each other's thoughts and feelings. Every day we work on building a relationship full of magical moments. This man has become the prince charming with whom I dreamed of living my love story. He is everything I once wrote on paper asking the universe for. He is chivalrous, romantic, attentive, intelligent, disciplined, tender, respectful, honest and, above all, always looking for a way to make me feel loved. He is funny, looks for the positive side of things, cares for me, worries about our future, makes me feel safe and offers me quality time. I think he is the man every good woman deserves to have. This relationship gives me peace, makes me feel loved and respected.

> " The folly of love is the greatest of heaven's blessings.
>
> PLATO

My dear, if you are going through difficult times with your partner, you do not feel loved or respected, and that person hurts you, I promise you that ending that relationship won't be the end of the world. There are good people out there, and if that relationship is hurting you the best thing to do is to end it. Give yourself time to work on your self-love, and when you do, you will see how wonderful people will start coming into your life. Don't be afraid to fall in love again, because, in the end, love always wins.

> " How you love yourself is how you teach others to love you.
>
> RUPI KAUR

During my life I went through depression in silence and got out of that hole, thinking life had no meaning. Today, after working on my self-love and self-knowledge, I can see life with the brightest colors I have ever seen. This is one of the many reasons I share my story and have created this book, to give you the tools that worked for me to move forward and reach the life you have always dreamed of.

It is vital to have a purpose and work on something that fills you with peace and happiness, we all grow with a gift and certain special abilities, look inside yourself and get that to become your life engine.

4

THE ART OF LOVING YOURSELF

Self-Love Exercises

DAY ONE

Dear, I am very happy to share this book with you. I want to show you everything I learned during this time of self-knowledge, where I sought to strengthen myself and fill myself with love. Together we will learn how self-love can create a better life for everyone. In this series of exercises and activities, you will learn some basic concepts to develop a positive and rewarding relationship with yourself. Although there are many exercises, I will show you which exercises helped me personally. First, you must understand what self-love means:

Self-love is the recognition and dignity of yourself, it means that you love yourself unconditionally, accept and honor your strengths and weaknesses, trust your abilities and work to improve your weak areas. With self-love, you will have a loving, lasting, healthy, and realistic relationship with yourself.

I want to clarify that I have learned these exercises during my life, through diplomas, courses, workshops, seminars, readings, psychological therapies, etc. I modified and updated most of these activities based on how they have worked for me personally, I hope they work for you, too. Remember, there is nothing better than going to a specialist, although you can do these exercises on your own. I will always recommend you put them into practice and go to psychological therapy. Going to therapy will help you see the world from a new perspective.

Next, we are going to do a few exercises that will help you begin this journey of self-knowledge.

1

Complete the following sentences. These statements will help you identify your strengths.

I love myself because _____
I love myself because _____
I love myself because _____

2

Once you have done this, now, make a list of your skills and accomplishments that make you unique, this will remind you of all the great things you have, and that you should be proud of.

Skills	Achievements

" Self-love begins and ends
with the dialogue we have
with ourselves.

KATHRYN EISMAN

3

Now is the time to create a personal goal. Think of something you would like to change or improve in your life, set realistic but challenging goals, and write them down in a visible place. This will remind you that it is possible to achieve what you set out to do and you will have confidence in your abilities to achieve it.

My personal goal is to _____

I will change my _____

I will improve my _____

My short-term goal is to _____

Date to meet short term objective __/__/__/__

My long-term goal is to _____

Date to meet long term objective __/__/__/__

4

In the following calendar, you will organize your schedule one day in advance. When you wake up, you will write down your goal, and at the end of the day, you will write down what you did to get closer to it. You should leave some free days during the week to do activities that give you pleasure and peace.

Time	M	T	Wednesday	Thursday	Friday	Saturday	Sunday
	Goal:	Goal:	Goal:	Goal:	Goal:	Goal:	
What brought me closer?							

My dear, trust yourself, don't compare yourself to other people's progress or processes. Each person is fighting their own internal battle, one that you know nothing about. Be kind to others, but especially to yourself. You are your main competition, focus on you and how to achieve it. Respect your body, your mind, and your spirit with small gestures every day, to make sure you are your best version. Self-love is the commitment to be on your side, to be your best friend, and most importantly, to be there for yourself unconditionally.

5

Activity to remind yourself how to love yourself.

You will set two alarms on your cell phone with five hours between them. Each time they ring you will ask yourself:

> What am I doing?
> What have I been thinking about myself in the last few hours?
> Are my thoughts useful?
> Am I self-sabotaging?
> Am I doubting myself?

Then, at that moment when you analyze your thoughts, you will read the following sentence: "I am my best friend, I love myself unconditionally, I respect myself, and I value myself".

Write this phrase in your notes on your phone or in the same reminder next to the alarms. Carry it with you always, so that when those thoughts come, you can read it and remember how wonderful you are.

" You are very powerful, as long as you know how powerful you are.

YOGI BHAJAN

6

Final activity

Now, take five minutes to write about your progress and reflect on what you are accomplishing, what makes you happy, what you have learned today and what you are grateful for.

Today__/__/__

_____

_____

_____

_____

_____

_____

_____

_____

_____

_____

SECOND DAY

Self-love is the key to self-confidence, happiness, and a deeper level of self-acceptance.

1

Do something you love to take you out of the monotony. This could be something as simple as taking an afternoon off to walk. What do you like to do? Read, sing, play an instrument, draw, dance, take a walk, listen to music, go to the movies, or get a massage. Write down what it is that gets you out of the monotony:

_____

_____

Now, commit to doing it at least twice a month.

I will do this on the __ day and also on the __ day of each month.

Remember that it is important to dedicate time to your body, exercise, eat healthy and maintain adequate hydration, this will help you feel good inside and out, thus raising your self-esteem.

2

Fill in the left box with five negative phrases, which make you feel bad based on your personality, and then on the right side, you will replace them with five phrases that are the positive side of the previous ones.

Negative	Positive

My dear, thoughts lead to emotions and emotions lead to reaction. It is an infinite circle that our brain performs. That's why I need you, when those negative thoughts appear, to ask yourself: "What do I accomplish by thinking that about myself, do I really believe that about myself?", and then, replace or modify them with positive phrases, for example, "I am enough, I love myself, I respect myself, I am my best friend, I can make it". As you modify those negative thoughts with positive ones, simultaneously, your life will begin to change around your positive actions. Your brain believes everything you say to it, so make sure you say nice things to it.

> " You are always with yourself,
> so enjoy your company.
>
> DIANE VON FURSTENBERG

3

Final activity

Now, take five minutes to write about your progress and reflect on what you are accomplishing, what makes you happy, what you have learned today and what you are grateful for.

Today__/__/__

_____

_____

_____

_____

_____

_____

_____

_____

_____

Recommended before going to sleep: place your cell phone away from you an hour before going to bed; this practice will help you disconnect from messages, notifications, and distractions, helping you calm your brain to rest better and have a pleasant sleep. If you have to use the alarm to wake up, this technique will also help you get up without postponing it.

THIRD DAY

Self-care and self-love are not about selfishness or excessive self-pity: they are about paying attention to our mental, emotional, and physical health, taking care of our needs for a healthy and happy life.

For today's activities, you must be in a private room with a mirror and your hands-free.

1

In front of the mirror look yourself straight in the eyes, and say three things you are proud of yourself for: you will start with your name and continue with each of the reasons you are proud of, they can be big or small things, for example:

I, Yeniffer, am proud because I stepped out of my comfort zone and wrote a book. I, Yeniffer, am proud because I floss my teeth.

I, Yeniffer, am proud to write frequently to my parents.
I, Yeniffer, am proud because I go out to sunbathe.
I, Yeniffer, am proud to be at my best today.

Now write it down and repeat it looking at yourself in the mirror.

I _____, am proud because _____.

I _____, am proud because _____.

I _____, am proud because _____.

2

Now tell yourself three things for which you forgive yourself while looking yourself in your eyes, such as:

I, Yeniffer, forgive myself because many times I didn't ask for help when I really needed it.

I, Yeniffer, forgive myself because I have thoughts that sabotage me.

I, Yeniffer, forgive myself for the times I have been too hard on myself.

Now write it down and repeat it looking at yourself in the mirror.

I _____, forgive myself for _____.

I _____, forgive myself for_____.

I _____, forgive myself for _____.

3

Looking you in the eye, again, you will say three sentences in which you commit yourself, such as:

I, Yeniffer, am committed to accepting my body as it is, with cellulite and imperfections.

I, Yeniffer, commit to telling myself positive phrases every day.

I, Yeniffer, commit to eating healthy every day.

I, Yeniffer, commit to engaging in physical activity every day.

Now write it down and repeat it looking at yourself in the mirror.

I _____, pledge _____.

I _____, pledge _____.

I _____, pledge _____.

Finally, remember that a good night's sleep is essential for your physical and mental health; you need to get adequate rest so that your body can recover from daily stress.

" Others only respect and love those who love themselves.

PAULO COELHO

4

Final activity

Now, take five minutes to write about your progress and reflect on what you are accomplishing, what makes you happy, what you have learned today, and what you are grateful for.

Today__/__/__/__

_____

_____

_____

_____

_____

_____

_____

_____

_____

_____

_____

FOURTH DAY

To practice self-care and self-love, it all starts with taking care of your mind. Recognizing positive and negative emotions is a healthy way to get to know yourself better.

Limit your time on social networks, as this will help you avoid comparison and decrease your anxiety, keeping negative ideas about yourself at bay. It is essential to keep in mind that self-love is directly linked to our thoughts. So, if you are encountering negative thoughts about yourself, I encourage you to transform those thoughts into kinder words and actions. This means being aware of those thoughts and reminding yourself that you are enough just as you are today. It is vital to learn to treat yourself with kindness. When we treat ourselves fairly, we give ourselves space to celebrate our victories, appreciate our unique qualities and motivate ourselves.

In today's exercise you will choose an activity that gives you peace, happiness, inspiration or connection with yourself, something that you like, but that takes time to finish: a painting, a choreography, a song, a physical training routine, a poem. After selecting one of these activities, you will divide the activity into thirty days until you finish it. As a final activity you will need to share it with someone special, for example: I, Yeniffer, decided to make a painting of a landscape and give it to my mother.

1

Choose the activity and write it down specifying your short and long-term goals. Example:

Activity: <u>paint a picture</u>.

Short-term action: <u>move forward each day in the painting, creating parts of the landscape</u>.

30-day goal: <u>finish it and give it to my mother</u>.

Activity:	
Short-term action:	
30-day target:	

This free time will help you connect with your inner self and express your creativity; it will teach you that whatever you set your mind to, you can achieve with patience and love.

> " Make a promise to yourself right now: declare that you are worthy of your time and energy.

DEBORAH DAY

2

Final activity

Now, take five minutes to write about your progress and reflect on what you are accomplishing, what makes you happy, what you have learned today and what you are grateful for.

Today__/__/__

_____

_____

_____

_____

_____

_____

_____

_____

_____

_____

_____

FIFTH DAY

It is essential to learn to say "no". Sometimes, the demands of others can overwhelm us, so listen to your voice and be aware of what you can handle. Choose people that make you feel good. The people you choose can influence how you feel about yourself. Making friends with positive, respectful people helps you maintain a good attitude. You can also practice "self-praise" by doing positive things for yourself, such as taking the afternoon off to rest, pampering yourself with a massage, or spending time with someone who makes you happy.

1

Today's exercise consists of answering the following questions:

To what or whom do I compare myself and why?

_____

_____

What do I feel is behind wanting others to like me?

_____

_____

What do I blame myself for?

_____

_____

Now you may be wondering:

What good does it do me to compare myself?

_____

_____

What good does it do me to worry about what they think of me?

_____

_____

Every time these thoughts come to you, keep in mind that everyone is different, everyone fights their own battles, everyone has different experiences, everyone invested a specific time to achieve a specific goal. No one is worse or better than anyone else, we are all growing and advancing as much as we can. Self-love is an integral part of self-care. Remember that you are a unique, wonderful being. Treat your mind and body with kindness and patience, avoid comparing yourself to others and try to build self-confidence. Use your self-praise, whether small or large, as fuel to reach your goals.

" A desire to be someone else would be a loss of the person I really am.

MARILYN MONROE

2

Final activity

Now, take five minutes to write about your progress and reflect on what you are accomplishing, what makes you happy, what you have learned today and what you are grateful for.

Today__/__/__

_____

_____

_____

_____

_____

_____

_____

_____

_____

_____

SIXTH DAY

Regular self-care and self-love helps us better connect with ourselves, strengthen our self-esteem, and make better life choices.

Today's activity will be a few minutes of meditation to connect with your inner self.

1

In a private room, sit on the floor with your legs crossed and your free hands touching your thighs, close your eyes, keep your body relaxed, draw a small smile on your face and start visualizing the following scenario:

Think that you are a being of light, your whole body is impregnated with a blue light that begins to rise through your toes, continues through your calves, continues through your knees, follows your thighs, then your hips, your genitals, your stomach, your chest, this light travels through your shoulders, arms, hands, up your neck until it reaches your face and continues infinitely to the sky.

This light brings health, strength, love, compassion, forgiveness, and purity. This light fills you with peace and happiness and whispers in your ear that you are enough, that you can achieve anything and everything you set your mind to, that now you are light and you can share that light with those you love. Embrace yourself, breathe deeply, slowly, and gently open your eyes.

With this activity you were able to connect with your inner self, I recommend you to do it every morning or before leaving home.

I'll leave with the audio of this activity below, so that you can do it comfortably without reading the text again. This is a private and free access that you as a reader of this book have. Go to the following *YouTube* link chapter 4, sixth day: https://youtu.be/lc5ghPON8J8

(THIS AUDIO IS TEMPORARILY NARRATED ONLY IN SPANISH).

" He who looks outside, dreams; he who looks inside, awakens.

CARL GUSTAV JUNG

2

Final activity

Now, take five minutes to write about your progress and reflect on what you are accomplishing, what makes you happy, what you have learned today and what you are grateful for.

Today__/__/__

_____

_____

_____

_____

_____

_____

_____

_____

_____

_____

_____

SEVENTH AND LAST DAY

Today, you will need to be in a private room. Sit comfortably, pay close attention, as you will use your senses for this activity. With your eyes, you will see each part of your body that I will be naming and with your hands, you will be touching them.

1

We start with the feet, calves, and thighs. Look at them, touch them and thank them, thank them for being strong and allowing you to walk, say: "Thank you for giving me the blessing of being able to get up every day, thank you for allowing me to walk, thank you for keeping me stable and not letting me fall". Now look at your stomach and chest, touch them, feel your heart, and say, "Thank you for keeping me alive, for allowing me to feed myself, digest my food, go to the bathroom, and pump my blood to keep my body and brain functioning properly." Touch your arms and hands, you can also smell yourself as you touch yourself, and say, "Thank you for allowing me to touch, thank you for allowing me to hug and to be able to hold things." Now touch every part of your face, and say, "Thank you for allowing me to breathe, feed, hear and see." Now hug yourself fully in the fetal position, and say, "Thank you to my body that strives every day to give me life and to make me a self-sufficient person. I thank myself because as of today I love myself unconditionally and I commit myself to be my best version and also to respect, value, love and praise myself, because I am enough, I am strong, I am love."

I leave you a link with the audio of this activity, so that you can do it comfortably without reading the text again. This is a private and free access that you as a reader of this book have.

Go to the following YouTube link for chapter 4, seventh day: https://youtu.be/lc5ghPON8J8

(THIS AUDIO IS TEMPORARILY NARRATED ONLY IN SPANISH).

> " Accepting ourselves as we are means valuing our imperfections as much as our perfections.

SANDRA BIERIG

Remember to put into practice all the activities you have learned. Applying these principles of self-care and self-love can change the course of your life. We all deserve a little love and care. If you continue to practice these critical areas of your life on a daily basis, you will soon be enjoying a mentally and emotionally healthy life. When you change your mind and your energy, it changes what you attract into your life.

2

Final activity

Now, take five minutes to write about your progress and reflect on what you are accomplishing, what makes you happy, what you have learned today and what you are grateful for.

Today__/__/__

_____

_____

_____

_____

_____

_____

_____

_____

_____

_____

5

AUTHOR'S NOTE

Dear, many times, we are surrounded by toxic and negative people in our lives. As a great advice I will tell you: the best thing you can do is to distance yourself from that kind of people, because believe it or not, energies greatly influence the way we see life. Your ideas can change if you change your friendships and personal relationships. As human beings, we are always in constant change, and that's okay, because it is part of our evolution.

- Change jobs if you don't feel comfortable with what you are being offered or with your work circle.

- Stay away from friendships or personal relationships that bring out the worst in you.

- Choose carefully because your environment will become you. You become what you surround yourself with. Energies are contagious.

- Break up with the love relationship that only exhausts you mentally and even more so if that relationship hurts you physically and psychologically.

- Get positive people, with thoughts of self-improvement, love, and honesty. It seems unbelievable, but your quality of life improves dramatically when you surround yourself with intelligent, good, positive, and kind people.

- If you finally cannot break up or separate yourself from certain people, because they are part of your family, the best thing to do is to keep your distance. We do not choose our family, but we cannot let ourselves be influenced.

- Give yourself the opportunity to go to therapy, to talk to a specialist, their only intention is to be there for you, to listen to you and help you. Psychologists and psychiatrists are there to help you get the solution to that problem you think you don't have.

- Never lose faith in yourself, no matter how hard and complicated life may seem, look around you, there will always be good people who can give you a hand.

- Trust in your abilities, believe in yourself, and remember that it is never too late to do what you want to do.

- Treat yourself with love and kindness, remember you are your best friend. You are the only one who can fix yourself and move on. I know that healing your heart can hurt a lot too, but I promise you that your well-being is worth every tear.

- Always be kind, because you can be the respite for someone who has a ton of anguish behind a smile. You have no idea how many people live painful realities in silence. Always remember that.

Dr. Mauricio Gonzalez, a specialist in obesity medicine, on his Instagram account (@dr.mauriciogonzalez) says: "Exercise is not a lifestyle suggestion, it is a biological demand. To date we know that, performing strength and aerobic exercise, is potentially related to the prevention and treatment of twenty-six common diseases in humans. It can increase the hippocampal neuronal population and promote more effective repair of our DNA. The how doesn't matter, it is irrelevant if you are dressed in the *trendiest outfit* of some brands, or in your pajamas. What matters is that you subject your body to the beneficial stress of exercise. You can do it at home or at the gym. Do it, that's what matters."

"Your beliefs become your thoughts, your thoughts become your words, your words become your actions, your actions become your habits, your habits become your values, your values become your destiny.", Mahatma Gandhi.

Dear, I hope you have enjoyed these self-love and self-care activities. Because you got this far, I want to give you a free consultation, so you can talk to a specialist, in case you have any concerns you want to work on. A psychologist will be there to listen to you. You are not alone.

To obtain this benefit, follow these steps:

1. Type in my personal Instagram account @yeniffergonzalezz (if you feel up to it, you can follow me, but that's optional).
2. In my last post, write, "I want to work on my best version."
3. Please wait. A specialist will contact you shortly.

This service (gift/consultation) will be available as long as I am able to maintain partnerships with health specialists or until the availability of the service is exhausted. (This service is temporarily available only in Spanish speaking). But, I will be working to get alliances in English, (you can write to me directly on my Instagram direct messages to help you).

I want to thank you for how much you would help me by sharing your opinion in the comment portal where you bought this book because it is crucial for me to help people like us who are going through difficult times and need support. Recommending this book or giving one to a friend, can change her life.

If you want to find out about new projects, products, conferences, interviews, events, and some other surprises, sign up on my web page: www.yeniffergonzalezz.com

> " Loving yourself is the beginning of a lifelong romance.

OSCAR WILDE

6

A LETTER TO MY FRIENDS

María Fernanda, or (as I called you when we were little): "Marifer", how could I ever forget when we played dolls, you were my best friend since I was three years old. You and your family became part of mine. We lived so many beautiful moments: like when your mom, whom I call Aunt Lola, would pick you up from kindergarten on a giant bicycle, and I would go with you, you and I together riding on the bar. Or when we would stop talking over silly things and fix it minutes later with a smile. Remember when we would go for empanadas for breakfast before we got to high school? At that fast food place on the corner of the public transportation stop. Those and many more memories are still in my mind. Even though we live in different countries, distance will never bring us apart.

Yosmary, I still remember when you took away my kindergarten lunch one day (ha, ha). You were a girl with a lot of character, but, gradually, you softened your heart to the point of becoming my friend. Together, Marifer, you and I grew up playing dolls, going to classes, talking about our first loves. Remember when we would go to Lorena and Mario's dance academy, and they would hire us to perform in public? Remember when you were a cupid between me and my first boyfriend? I want you to know that I loved sharing our lives and I still treasure those beautiful memories.

Suleika, Geilibeth and Raul, remember our dance group, Class 406, like the youth series of that time (ha, ha, ha). I remember how popular we were, how much fun we had dancing and creating choreographies. It was a very nice time; ad incredible moments that I will never forget.

Fellow students of the Angel Quintero School, thank you for having been part of such a beautiful stage, I remember each one of you with great affection.

Yohaiver, I hope you remember when we used to go to the field in front of our houses. We would go out with a notebook, pen, and a magnifying glass that I don't remember where I got (ha, ha, ha). We thought we were Boy Scouts and would look for butterfly cocoons to watch them grow. You were my first best friend, I always loved spending time with you, always with a big beautiful smile, remember when I taught you to eat tomato and cucumber with flavored cube, soy sauce and lemon (ha, ha, ha).

Friends of the José Antonio Chávez High School, there were many of you with whom I shared unique moments, with some I went to the beach, with others I shared the discipline club, others were my study group – we add a healthy competition going – and with others I shared the environmental club. I remember the last year of classes, we said goodbye by going on a trip and we had a lot of fun on the way, dancing, listening to music, joking, taking pictures, and sharing knowledge with the geography teacher. I take with me beautiful memories of all of you, my classmates and teachers who made that stage a wonderful experience.

Friends from the University of Zulia "Luz" with whom I studied Geodesic Engineering. I still remember when they surprised me with a chocolate cake and signs for my eighteenth birthday. How could I forget that they filled my face with cake (ha, ha, ha). With you I shared that magical, but at the same time complicated stage. My first tears of frustration for not understanding calculus, algebra, and geometry (ha, ha, ha). Do you still remember when we went to the movies on Fridays after class?

Friends and professors of UNIR, what can I say to you! Thank you for your love and support, thank you for encouraging me to believe in myself. You were a very important part of my professional growth. And if it had not been for you, who insisted me so much to participate in that institutional beauty contest, I would not have lived as many wonderful experiences as the ones I lived after winning that contest. Thank you. I hope you still remember when, to celebrate the end of our term, we went to eat *pizza* in the Saladillo neighborhood.

Ricardo, thank you, because from the day I met you, you were always there for me unconditionally. I will never forget when you would pick me up at my house after my cosmetic surgery to take me to my therapies and appointments. Nor will I forget how you looked at me with loving eyes, even while my face was all bruised, with bands and a cast on my nose, you told me that even with bruises on my eyes, I still looked beautiful. You really taught me that beauty does not come from the body, but from the heart.

Jeudiel, thank you for teaching me that true friends support each other in difficult moments without expecting anything in return. You were my relief in a stormy moment.

To my makeup artists, stylists, designers, and representatives, I thank you for believing in my potential even before I did it myself; for helping me highlight my qualities to achieve my goals, thank you.

Faddya and Priscila, after we met in Miami, we became great friends. To you, thank you for being there. Thank you for driving long distances to visit me or even for taking a plane. Thank you for teaching me that even though we have busy lives and live long distances apart, I can always count on you. Faddya, thank you for teaching me the true meaning of the word friend, you supported me and accompanied me in many beautiful moments. Priscila, I still remember when you and your whole family went to support me in my first fashion show in Miami. You two formed the most beautiful stage of my life I could have lived in Florida. Thank you.

Lucero, Melissa, and Blanca, although they are three opposite personalities, if there is one thing, I have to thank for moving to Los Angeles, it is having met you. You form my current circle of friends, you are the ones with whom I have shared my last years, we have traveled, celebrated, cried, and grown together, I am so grateful to life for having put you on my path! I thank them for filling me with so much love. Lucero, how could I forget when we met working at Porto's Bakery, after that, we have shared extraordinary moments. Melissa, who would have thought that after two brothers broke our hearts, we would become inseparable friends. Thank you for making me the aunt of a beautiful prince. Blanca, I hope you never forget our adventures when we were working at the Amazon "KSBD" airport where we couldn't stop laughing in between jokes, or when we planned a wonderful trip to Seattle and were caught in the snow and the car slipped as we drove up the hills. I hope my influence in getting you into the U.S. Army gives you great experiences and the life you always wanted to live. Girls, truly, thank you for staying in my life, I love you.

Many people have left a mark on me: unforgettable moments, memories that I carry in my heart. To all of you, wonderful people who accompanied me in my best and worst moments, and whom I once called my angels, thank you for having been there for me and, although many of us have distanced ourselves for different reasons, I will always carry you in my heart.

A LETTER TO MY FAMILY

Mom, you always give more than you receive, you have the noblest and kindest heart I know. I am sorry because, many times, I did not know how to value your efforts. You worked tirelessly to feed us, and that had the consequence of leaving us in the care of my great-grandmother; you did not know that we would receive so much mistreatment from her. Although the way you raised us was not the right way, I want you to know that I do not blame you for leaving us with her. I know that, from your heart, you longed to share time with us. I also know that in your childhood, you suffered a lot, and that as an adult you did the best you could with what you had, at that time. Although the time we shared was short, it was enough to show me the purest and truest love I had ever known. You taught me that a mother's love can be the world's strongest and most valuable power. Thank you because, as I grew up, you became my best friend. I still remember when I was five years old and you would get up very early to get me dressed and send me to kindergarten with transportation, tears running down my cheeks because I knew I wouldn't see you again until the next day. And when you would come home early from work, I would run out to hug you. I remember how your smile would light up your face, your perfect golden curls would sway in the wind and your honey-colored eyes would make me sigh. Nor will I forget that time in college when I came back to live with you, how you lovingly woke me up with a kiss and a cup of coffee to watch the sunrise together. I hope I can always show you how much I love you and how proud I am to be your daughter.

Dad, I longed for more love, understanding and attention from you while I was growing up. That support that any child needs from a father. Your absence hurt me at many stages of my life. It hurt not seeing you at my kindergarten graduation. Years later, I held out hope that you would show up at my high school graduation, but you never came. In the year I moved in with you, I was given an award for best academic average, and I saw all the parents accompanying their children, except mine. Later I lost hope and decided not to invite you to my bachelor's graduation ceremony. You were so absent from my childhood to my Teenage Years that I had a hard time overcoming that pain. Although you never apologized for your mistakes, I want you to know I forgave you long ago. But, I also ask for your forgiveness, because later I understood that your life was not easy either, that nobody taught you how to be a good father. That from your ignorance you did the best that was in your hands. I want to tell you that, although I remember the past, it no longer hurts me, because I healed my heart. I keep those beautiful memories of when we were kids and you took us to the beach, or when you took us to your house, rented movies and prepared our meals (one day you rented *The Sword in the Stone*, of the wizard Merlin and King Arthur, it became my favorite movie because it links that beautiful memory of me lying on your chest while we watched it). As an adult, do you remember when you used to take me to my beauty pageant rehearsals, do you remember that last trip to Curaçao? I learned that, although the past may hurt, it is my decision to heal and build a more beautiful present. I love you.

Grandma Inés, I lack words to explain my love and gratitude for you. You taught me most of the principles and values that I carry in my heart. You taught me true unconditional love. Thank you for educating me, giving me so much love, for your advice and blessings, and for still being there for me. I will never forget all the moments we shared, like when we slept together and you told me your interesting life stories, until I fell asleep. I still remember when as a child you gave me a *Barbie* with a closet full of closets, I loved that *Barbie* so much! Do you remember when I used to fall down in kindergarten as a child? I would always come home with bumps on my forehead, and you would stuff my face with menthol to ease the pain. In the end, my eyes would burn more from the menthol than the pain of the bump itself (ha, ha, ha). I love you with all my heart.

Brother JJ, we shared so many moments, endless adventures, and stories. We were like soul mates. I remember how we laughed non-stop, as a child you were my best friend and confidant. Even though we live in different countries, and you are already the father of two beautiful girls, I want you to know that I still see you as I did when we were six and nine years old. I admire you for becoming a good man, for breaking patterns and creating a family full of love. I love you.

To the rest of my family, maternal and paternal, I want to say never forget how much I love you, I will never tire of telling you. And although I was not the one who chose you as my family at birth, if I could in another life choose you, I would certainly do it again. Even though we have all been through some tough times, we will always support each other and showering each other with love. We are not the perfect family, but you are the family I love to have. I want to name them all in this book, but there are so many (ha, ha, ha).

To my parents, brothers, sisters, grandmothers, grandfather, aunts, uncles, cousins, cousins, to all of you, thank you for making my life a school of beautiful experiences. I love you.

" Every time you hate, a part of you is destroyed. Every time you forgive, you heal yourself.

WALTER RISO

Naty, Kevin and Paul, thank you for opening the doors to your home and adopting me as part of your family. Thank you for believing in me, for supporting me and pushing me to grow. Thank you for being that family that I needed so much outside abroad. You taught me that a family does not necessarily have to be of the same blood. Thank you for so much unconditional love.

Dear reader, of course I want to thank you too. Thank you for supporting me and reading my first book, thank you for wanting to be a better version of yourself and those around you.

7

MY CURRENT ROUTINE

Dear, I share with you my daily routine; doing these activities make my days have sense and order. Maybe this will help you too.

- I have the habit of waking up with the sunlight coming through my window. I don't like alarms; I feel my heart and ears explode when I hear them.
- I go to the bathroom, do my physiological needs: brush my teeth (I look in the mirror and tell myself some positive and motivational phrases), put on my clothes to go to the gym and comb my hair.
- I return to the room to spread out the bed.
- I go to the kitchen, prepare my breakfast, and weigh my meals. I use an app to log my food for the day (this helps me know the calories and nutrients I consume).
- Breakfast (I try to be more conscious, chew slowly, pay attention to the smells, textures, and flavors of my food).
- I review my activities that I scheduled the day before in my iPhone reminders.

- I prepare the protein to take with me and then take it when I leave the gym.
- I go to the *gym*, train (depending on the day: weights and/or cardio), and while I do it, I listen to music, *podcasts*, or an audiobook.
- I return to my car and drink protein on the way home.
- I get home, take a shower, and get dressed comfortably.
- I write to my parents and my grandmother.
- I take my vitamins (A, D, C, E, biotin, collagen, and multivitamin).
- I sit in my office and start working on my projects/undertakings. (Before starting any project, I do my best to write down my short-, medium- and long-term goals; doing that practice makes my daily activities easier and helps me a lot with the progress to achieve my goals).
- I prepare my lunch, reweigh, and record the food.
- I return to the office to dedicate many hours to my studies and *online* psychology classes, almost the rest of the day.
- I prepare dinner, weigh, and record the food.
- I take a shower, brush my teeth.
- I go to bed, sit comfortably, grab my journal (*iPhone* notes), and write about my day, my feelings and some ideas that have occurred to me.
- I schedule my activities for the next day in my *iPhone* reminders.
- I read a little bit of a book (my favorites are personal growth books).
- And I go to sleep.

None of my activities have specific schedules because, nowadays, I have a very flexible lifestyle. I usually schedule my activities a day in advance and that helps me be more organized and not to forget the things I have to do the next day. Not every day is the same; I also alternate between self-care and *mindfulness* routines. Some days of the month I have an appointment with my therapist. And when my boyfriend is home, my routine usually changes, as I prioritize spending quality time with him.

If you are curious about how I do any of my activities, you can follow me on my social networks and ask me any questions in the comments of my publications. I will be happy to answer you.

And finally, my dear, I leave you with the importance of mental and physical health for me: going to therapy and exercising goes beyond a superficial appearance, it is a discovery of all the potential within me. It is understanding that if my head is not well nothing will be; it is increasing my self-esteem; it is learning to value my process; it is doing the best I can to live in the present; it is understanding that after healing I will no longer be the same, now I will be a better version of me. And of course, it will hurt, there will be good days and not so good days. Feeling frustrated, angry, stressed, or disappointed is part of the process, but I am sure it is worth every tear!

8

ABOUT THE AUTHOR

Yeniffer Rossana González Molero, faithful believer of the phrase: "Be whoever you want to be", was born on July 1, 1993, in the city of Maracaibo, Zulia State, Venezuela. She is a psychology student at the Universidad Bicentenaria de Aragua in Venezuela. She is the author of the books: Querida yo el arte de amarte (original version in Spanish); Diario práctico 365 días para amarme; Bilingual book for children Color your self-esteem. She has studied some course, diplomas and seminars related to: Interventions to combat depression; introduction to clinical sexology and sex therapy; Autism in early childhood; introduction to couples therapy; Symposium in clinical psychology and therapeutic tools; Mindfulness as a therapeutic tool; Bipolar affective disorder approach in mental health; Understanding the clinical characteristics of ADHD; Stories, stories as clinical tools in psychotherapy; Safety plan for suicidal crises; Use of brief cognitive *tests*: clinical, neuropsychological and psychometric considerations.

In her thirties, she has achieved the following academic and professional merits: Graduated as a university technician in administration. With diplomas in: Business Management; Accounting; Digital Marketing; Nursing Assistant; International Cuisine; Healthy Cuisine.

In her career as a beauty queen, she achieved the following merits: Winner of the institutional contest Miss UNIR, she obtained the titles "Miss UNIR 2014" and "Miss Elegance 2014". Winner in the regional contest of the state of Zulia, Miss Nor Occidental, she obtained the titles "Miss Nor Occidental 2015" and "Chica Garbo 2015". As an official candidate of Miss Venezuela, she obtained the titles "Miss Zulia 2015", "Miss Venus Legs 2015" and "Top 10 Finalist of Miss Venezuela 2015". Winner in the CN Models International Search contest in Ecuador, she obtained the titles "Best Face 2017" And was winner of the CN Models International Search EFW 2017". Winner of the Dama Diamante contest in Miami, Florida, she obtained the title "Dama Diamante Miami 2018".

In her career as a runway model, she paraded for several international designers and brands.

> " Without darkness, there would be no light. Without storms, there would be no rainbows. And without rain, there would be no flowers.
>
> YENIFFER GONZALEZ

You can contact me on social media at:

Instagram: Yeniffergonzalezz
TikTok: Yeniffergonzalezz1
www.yeniffergonzalezz.com

These are my personal accounts, so, don't freak out if you see things you weren't expecting (ha, ha, ha). Remember that *"judging a person doesn't define who they are, it defines who you are."*

9

BIBLIOGRAPHY

Dear Reader, I want to share with you the readings that influenced my way of thinking and seeing life. These have accompanied me in my growth.

No es cuestión de leche, es cuestión de actitud. Carlos Saúl Rodríguez

¿Quién se ha llevado mi queso? Spencer Johnson, M.D.

La culpa es de la vaca. Jaime Lopera and Marta Inés Bernal

Desapegarse sin anestesia. Walter Riso.

Las siete leyes espirituales del éxito. Deepak Chopra

Comer, Rezar, Amar. Elizabeth Gilbert

Síntesis de la sabiduría espiritual. Kaled Yorde

El alquimista. Paulo Coelho

El código de las mentes extraordinarias. Vishen Lakhiani

Los hombres son de Marte, las mujeres son de Venus. John Gray

El poder de los pensamientos positivos. Norman Vincent Peale

Cómo hacer que te pasen cosas buenas. Marian Rojas Estape

La tienda de magia. James R. Doty

El poder del ahora. Eckhart Tolle

El club de las 5 de la mañana. Robin Sharma

Los 7 hábitos de la gente altamente efectiva. Stephen R. Covey

Los cuatro acuerdos. Dr. Miguel Ruiz

El monje que vendió su Ferrari. Robin Sharma

El secreto. Rhonda Byrne

Inteligencia emocional. Daniel Goleman

Padre rico, padre pobre. Robert T. Kiyosaki

Enamórate de ti. Walter Riso

Encuentra tu persona vitamina. Marian Rojas Estapé